CHINA FOCUS

CHANGING CHINA

Edited by Marta Segal Block

Heinemann Library
Chicago, Illinois

Customer Service   888–454–2279

Visit our website at www.heinemannlibrary.com

Designed by Richard Parker and Manhattan Design
Printed by China Translation Printing Services

12 11 10 09 08
10 9 8 7 6 5 4 3 2 1

Library of Congress Cataloging-in-Publication Data
Block, Marta Segal.
   China focus : changing China / Marta Segal Block.
       p. cm.
   Includes bibliographical references and index.
   ISBN-13: 978-1-4329-1217-8
   1. China--Juvenile literature. I. Title.
   DS706.B565 2008
   951--dc22

                                    2007049476

Acknowledgments
The publishers would like to thank the following for permission to reproduce photographs:
©Alamy (Lewton Cole) p. **13**; ©Camera Press pp. **20, 24**; ©Corbis pp. **7** (Royalty Free), **10** (Royal Ontario Museum), **15** (Adrian Bradshaw), **16** (David Turnley), **17** (Bettmann), **21** (Eye Ubiquitous/ Patrick Field), **22** (Lawrence Manning), **23** (Reuters), **28** (Democratic Voice of Burma), **29** (Michael Freeman), **31** (Richard Wainwright), **32** (George Tiedemann), **37** (Mike Kemp), **38** (Reuters/Lucas Jackson), **39** (epa/Srdjan Suki), **40** (Stephanie Maze); ©Getty Images pp. **8** (DAJ), **9** (IZA Stock), **12** (Hulton Archive), **19** (Hulton Archive), **30** (Kristian Dowling), **33** (AFP/Mark Ralston), **35** (AFP/Karen Bleier), **41** (Stone); ©Pearson Education Ltd pp. **18** (Debbie Rowe), **36** (Gareth Boden); ©Peter Newark American Pictures p. **14**; ©Photolibrary pp. **4** (Jon Arnold Images), **34** (Imagestate Ltd).

Cover photograph of office blocks in Pudong, Shanghai, China, reproduced with permission of ©Getty Images (Photographer's Choice).

The publisher would like to thank Julie McCulloch, David Downing, Neil Morris, and Tony Allan for additional material.

Every effort has been made to contact copyright holders of any material reproduced in this book. Any omissions will be rectified in subsequent printings if notice is given to the publisher.

Contents

Some words are printed in bold, **like this**. You can find out what they mean by looking in the glossary.

Why China Is Important

The large size of the country and the number of people who live there make China very important to the world, **economically** and **politically**. China's **culture** also is important to the world. China has one of the oldest civilizations. Many of the foods we eat and items that we use every day were first discovered or invented in China.

Throughout its history, China has had a reputation for being **isolated** and disapproving of foreigners. Today, as communications and **technology** make travel and business between countries easier, that reputation is changing.

The Dragon Boat Festival has been celebrated in China since 300 BCE. This is just one example of China's long-surviving culture.

CULTURE AND CIVILIZATION

Any group of people can be said to have a culture. If your school has school colors, a school song, or certain traditions, this is all part of your school's culture. A civilization is the group that practices the culture. When we say that China has one of the oldest civilizations, we mean that traditions such as songs, art, and religion have been passed from person to person throughout China for thousands of years.

China is large and growing larger. All the colored areas on this map show the whole of China.

CHINESE LANGUAGE

In Chinese, words are written using symbols or characters, rather than letters. There are several different **dialects** of Chinese spoken throughout the country. The standard language is known as putonghua (common era language). English speakers often refer to this as Mandarin Chinese. Since Chinese is written differently from English, you often will see Chinese words spelled differently in different places. Sometimes, the words will look so different that they seem to not even be the same words. For example, the city of Beijing, China's capital, used to be spelled Peking in English. This book uses a system called Pinyin to write Chinese words. This is the Chinese government's preferred way of writing Chinese words in English letters.

China's government

China is a **totalitarian** or **authoritarian** state. This means that the government is all-powerful and does not have to listen to the people. The government is ruled by the Chinese **Communist** Party. Almost every top job in the country is held by a member of this party. In China today, however, two of the government ministers (for health and science) are not members of the Communist Party. As we will see, this is a departure from the traditions of Communism and the Chinese Communist Party. It shows that the government may be becoming more open to discussion and disagreement.

The Chinese people lack many political and social freedoms that people in **democratic** countries take for granted. Traditionally, in Communist countries the government controls more than just politics. The government controls all forms of expression. People are not allowed to write books, plays, or movies that the government does not like. The newspapers and TV news also must support the government. Having these policies helps keep the government in control.

A famous Chinese quote says: "The empire, long united, must divide; long divided, must unite. Thus it has always been." Throughout its history, the country of China has united and divided many times. Changes have been made, remade, and undone. Will this trend continue today? In order to decide, it is important to know a little bit about China's past.

The Chinese flag is similar to the flag of the former **Soviet Union**. The large star in the upper left corner symbolizes the Communist party. The four smaller stars represent the four main groups in society: peasants, workers, the middle class, and merchants.

Chinese History

China is one of the world's oldest countries. Its recorded history goes back more than 4,000 years. For centuries, China was ruled by different families. These families were known as **dynasties**. The time of the ruling dynasties is known as **Imperial** China.

The Great Wall of China

The Great Wall of China is one of the world's largest, and oldest, structures. In 221 BCE, China's first **emperor** joined existing sections of the wall together to build a barrier to the outside world. Later, the wall began to fall apart. During the Ming Dynasty (1368), the wall was rebuilt. Since then, parts of the wall have crumbled, but large sections of it remain. The wall is 4,500 miles (7,300 kilometers) long.

The Great Wall was built to keep out foreigners. Today, visitors from around the world are allowed to visit and walk on sections of the wall.

ABOUT DATES

In Western culture, dates usually are given as either BCE (sometimes written as BC) or CE (sometimes written as AD). The term BCE stands for "before the common era." These dates often seem "backward." The year 5 BCE is a date five years before the start of the common era. The year 10 BCE happened before the year 5 BCE.

The Chinese have two different calendars. The traditional calendar may have been in use for more than 4,000 years. Legends say it started during the Xia Dynasty, but this has not been proved. This calendar is used to figure out the dates of holidays, such as the Chinese New Year and other important events. However, the Chinese also use the Gregorian Calendar (the calendar you use). The Gregorian Calendar is known as the official calendar.

The traditional Chinese calendar sometimes is called the Yin Calendar or the agricultural calendar.

CHINESE LITERATURE

Stories, poems, and songs always have been important in China. China's most famous poet is Li Bai (also known as Li Po). He lived in the 700s and wrote about nature and friendship. Thousands of his poems survive and are still studied in school. Many older works also survive and are studied. Until the early 1900s, Chinese literature was written in an ancient language that only some people could read. Under the early Communist rulers, **censorship** meant that only some works were published. Today, a greater variety of writing is available.

China before 1900

Although today's Communist government officially disapproves of China's former dynasties, they are a very important part of Chinese culture. China did not come under foreign rule until 1279, when the people from Mongolia invaded. One of the most famous Chinese dynasties was the Ming, who ruled from 1368–1644. The Ming Dynasty was famous for its relationships with other countries. In the 1400s, China began exploring areas as far away as India and Africa. In 1514, the first Portuguese ships reached China.

These vases are from the Ming and Qing dynasties. For hundreds of years, no one outside of China knew how these beautiful vases were made.

There were several "Silk Roads" between China and Europe. Traders brought materials and ideas from place to place.

Black Sea

Caspian Sea

Aral Sea

Gobi Desert

N
W—E
S

Antioch

Mediterranean Sea

Ecbatana

Merv

Kashgar

Taklamakan Desert

Khotan

Dunhang

Xian

CHINA

INDIA

Silk Road
Desert
Mountains

0   500 miles

0   1000 km

THE SILK ROAD

China has been trading with other countries for centuries. The Silk Road was a famous trade route that brought Chinese silk and spices to other countries, and horses and materials back to China. Even religion traveled over the Silk Road. **Buddhism** developed in northeastern India. It first was brought to China during the Han Dynasty (206 BCE—220 CE). By the 600s, Buddhism had become an important religious practice. The Silk Road remained an important trade route until the 1700s. In the 1960s, tourists began traveling the routes. Today, there are still tours of the routes. These tours mean that ideas and values continue to be traded from country to country.

China 1900–1949

In the 1800s, Europe started to become more and more interested in China and its resources. China's emperors had referred to China as "The Middle Kingdom," meaning that China was the center of the world. By the 1900s, however, China was no longer the center of the world. In fact, it was not even seen as a very important place. In the West, the **Industrial Revolution** was changing the way countries worked and traveled. China however, did not change.

At first, China's factories did not become modern as quickly as factories in the rest of the world. Today, China is known for its modern technology.

The Boxer Rebellion

By the 1900s, a series of **famines**, humiliations, and defeats had left the Chinese people angry. In the 1890s, China and Japan began fighting over neighboring Korea. In 1900, China was defeated by the Japanese. Gangs of Chinese youth joined an underground **revolutionary** movement known as the Fists of Righteous Harmony. The Boxers, as the rebels became known, practiced a secret form of martial arts that they claimed could magically protect them from bullets.

The Boxers took control of Beijing and the imperial government secretly lent its support. Several nations, including the United States, Britain, Germany, France, Russia, and Japan, sent troops to defeat the rebels. This was the only time the great powers of the day worked together. Even today, China often sees itself as being one country working against the rest of the world.

The West

When people talk about "The West" or "Western culture" they usually mean the countries located in North America and Western Europe. Countries like the United States, the United Kingdom, France, and Germany all share some parts of their culture. "The East" generally refers to the countries of Asia.

Cello player Yo Yo Ma was born in Paris, France, to Chinese parents. The cello is seen as part of Western culture, but Yo Yo Ma plays both Eastern and Western music on it. The cultures of the East and West are coming closer together, because of people like Yo Yo Ma.

A new country

On January 1, 1912, The Republic of China was officially declared. China's age of dynasties was at an end. Unfortunately, the fighting was not. Two groups, the **Nationalists** and Communists, at first worked together to make changes in the new country. Both groups were interested in giving more power to the common people.

However, by the late 1920s, differences between the two parties were starting to become clear. By 1927, the two political parties were no longer allies, they were enemies. For a time, the Nationalist party was in charge. The Communists were driven into hiding.

СЛАВА ВЕЛИКОМУ КИТАЙСКОМУ НАРОДУ,
ЗАВОЕВАВШЕМУ СВОБОДУ, НЕЗАВИСИМОСТЬ И СЧАСТЬЕ!

This Soviet poster celebrates the victory of the Communist party in China. As the world's leading Communist power, the Soviet Union welcomed the arrival of the new Communist country. Later, the two countries would have a falling out.

The two groups continued to fight each other. On October 1, 1949, Mao Zedong, the leader of the Communists, announced the start of the People's Republic of China. This announcement was made at the Gate of Heavenly Peace, where new dynasties were announced centuries ago. The remaining members of the Nationalist party fled to the island of Taiwan. In Taiwan, they set up a separate government. The relationship between the government in Taiwan, and the government in China, is still an issue today.

Taiwan is famous not only for its beauty, but also for its industry.

The Changing Government and Economy

The Chinese government now wants to have a Communist government, but a Western-style, **market-based economy**. The countries of the West want China to become a democracy, but also want to do business with China. Western governments know that if they push the Chinese government too hard about becoming a democracy, they will lose the ability to do business in China. The struggle between all these different desires is responsible for many of the changes China is undergoing currently.

In 1989, hundreds of students who were protesting against the Chinese government were killed by the Chinese Army in Tiananmen Square. This photograph shows the aftermath of the violence. Although Western governments disapproved of what happened, they had to be careful in what they said so as not to lose China's business.

Karl Marx is considered to be the father of Communism.

COMMUNISM AND CAPITALISM

Communism is a political movement based on the writings of Karl Marx. Marx believed that people should be treated equally, no matter what they did for a living. In a **capitalist** economy, the government interferes as little as possible with the way businesses are run. Capitalists believe that buyers and sellers together will decide how much things should cost. Buyers and sellers also decide how much people should be paid. This is what is meant by a market-based economy. In a Communist country, however, the government controls such things.

China's economy

For hundreds of years, the Chinese economy was based in agriculture. **Peasants** worked in the rice fields to feed themselves, and very few people lived in the cities. In the 1950s, when the Communist government took over, China began very quickly to have an economy that relied more and more on **industry**. This meant that people began to move away from the countryside and into the city.

The new government tried to use modern techniques for farming. These decisions often were made by people who did not fully understand either farming or the new technology. Rules that made little sense were passed, because people were not allowed to disagree with the government.

The Chinese have been growing rice in difficult places, such as mountainsides, for centuries.

HONG KONG

In 1898, China and Britain signed an agreement that Britain would control the island of Hong Kong for 99 years. Since Hong Kong was run by Britain, a capitalist country, it too had a capitalist economy. In 1997, Britain had to return Hong Kong to China. The two countries made a special agreement that Hong Kong would keep its capitalist system for 50 years. Because of these special agreements, Hong Kong seems very different than the rest of China. The people who live there are used to more freedoms, and the city seems more like a western city than a Chinese one.

Among other things, Hong Kong is famous for its movie industry. Many action and comedy movies are made in Hong Kong. The actors Jackie Chan and Jet Li got their start in Hong Kong movies and have brought the action styles of these movies to Hollywood movies.

Deng Xiaoping

Mao Zedong died in 1976. He had led China for more than 20 years, and the country was in shock at his death. He was followed as leader by Deng Xiaoping. Deng was famous for believing that results were more important than following rules.

Deng Xiaoping became China's leader in 1976.

The Four Modernizations

In 1978, Deng introduced a program known as the Four Modernizations. The four areas to be made more modern were industry, defense, technology, and agriculture. The first priority was agriculture. The program in this area was very successful and food production grew.

Deng also began to let foreign countries into China to give advice, and money. In 1979, Deng created Special Economic Zones, which made it easier for foreign countries to do business in China. China's large population, all possible customers, made this attractive to other countries.

Under Deng, Western goods were allowed in to China.

This poster advertises the benefits of families having only one child.

计划生育是我国的一项基本国

FAMILY PLANNING—A BASIC NATIONAL POLICY OF CHINA

China's one child policy

Some years after Deng came to power, China's population hit 1 billion people. Deng realized that living standards could not improve if the number of people in the nation grew faster than its resources. He decided to reduce the growth rate.

In 1979, Deng launched a campaign to restrict families to one child. Families that had more children, except under special circumstances, were punished by fines and lost some health and education benefits. The policy cut the **birth rate** by almost half. The policy was very unpopular in the countryside, where large families were needed to work the land.

Today, the policy is seen as being partly responsible for some of the changes in China's culture. Some people believe that the single children are valued so highly by their parents that they have become spoiled. They also believe the focus has shifted from respect for elders to worshipping of children. The policy shows how culture, politics, and the economy all are tied together. Changes in any one part of a society can have effects in other areas.

A 21st-century economy

By 2007, China was the second-largest economy in the world after the United States. Today, it **exports** more goods than it **imports**. Agriculture still is an important part of the economy, and probably will continue to be so. In 2000, China was the world's largest producer and user of rice and wheat. However, industry is becoming far more important.

Rice still is picked by hand, a difficult job.

China's growing economy has caused it to change some of its former political views, especially when it comes to other countries. For example, China and Japan once were bitter enemies, but today the two neighbors trade with each other. In 2001, China joined the **World Trade Organization**, showing its plans to continue working with other countries.

Around 1,500 people were infected with SARS in 2003.

Some things remain the same

The opening of the Chinese economy has meant that the government has had to make itself more open to other countries. However, this change has not been complete. In 2002, there was an outbreak in China of the deadly disease **SARS**. The Chinese government tried to keep the problem quiet. Not only were they unsuccessful, but their failure to report the disease to the outside world made the problem worse. Since China was not honest about the problem, people traveled from China, spreading the disease to other places.

The environment

Many of China's changes have come with a heavy price. Factories stand where fields once were, spilling poisons into the air. China is now famous for its pollution and smog. Rates of cancer and other diseases are going up. In democratic countries such as the United States, the people's protest can help force the government to fix these problems. Since protests are not allowed in China, it is hard to force the government to make changes.

China's Place in the World

For much of its history, China was isolated from the rest of the world by geography and politics. But through the 1900s and since 2000, China's importance in the world has changed and grown.

The leading Communist country

By the time Mao Zedong declared the People's Republic of China in 1949, the Soviet Union was considered the leading power in the Communist world. The Soviet Union, or USSR, had been a Communist country since 1917.

At first, the two countries were close allies. Many of Mao's policies followed Russian examples. He also used Russian advisers. However, by the late 1950s, some of Mao's policies had changed. By the 1960s, China and the Soviet Union were no longer close allies. In 1960, the Soviet Union stopped sending economic help to China. China began to strengthen ties with its former enemy, the United States.

Soviet leader Nikita Khrushchev and Mao Zedong shake hands in 1954, when relations between the two countries were still strong.

At that time, the United States and the Soviet Union disagreed on many issues. The United States wanted China to end its relationship with the Soviet Union. Until 1971, the United States had seen the government on the island of Taiwan as China's official government. But in 1971, the United States started recognizing the government on mainland China as China's official government. This helped China become closer to the United States, and less close to the Soviet Union.

In the late 1980s and early 1990s, the Soviet Union began to **collapse**. By 1991, there was not a Communist country left in Europe. This left China as the undisputed leader of the Communist world.

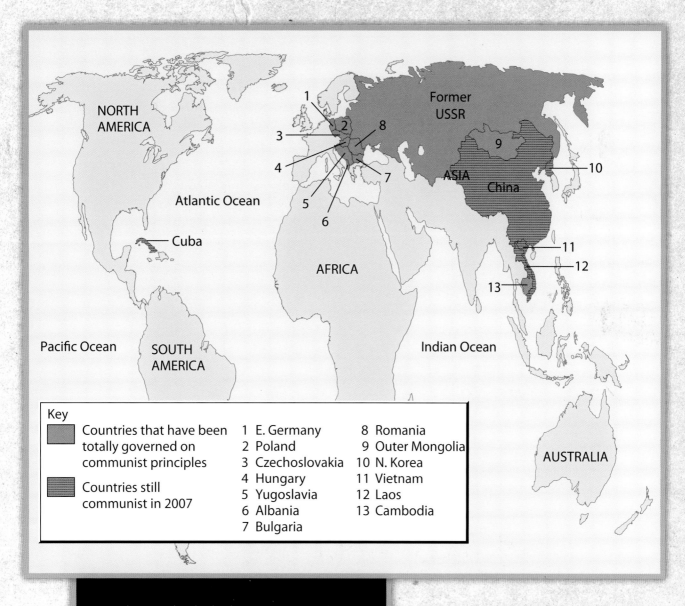

Key

| ▨ | Countries that have been totally governed on communist principles |
| ▤ | Countries still communist in 2007 |

1 E. Germany
2 Poland
3 Czechoslovakia
4 Hungary
5 Yugoslavia
6 Albania
7 Bulgaria
8 Romania
9 Outer Mongolia
10 N. Korea
11 Vietnam
12 Laos
13 Cambodia

China is clearly the largest Communist country in the world today.

China and Japan

China and Japan are the two largest and most powerful countries in Asia. They have had a long, and often difficult relationship. China has had a large influence on Japan's writing, religion, and culture. However, the two countries have not always gotten along.

The first recorded battle between the two countries was in the year 663. This battle also involved Korea. For many hundreds of years, China, Japan, and Korea continued to fight with different results. In 1894, Japan defeated China and took over control of the island of Taiwan. Japan participated in the Boxer Rebellion on the side of the European powers. In 1931, Japan occupied Manchuria, renaming it Manchukuo. During World War II, China was allied with the powers of the United States, France, Russia, and Britain, while Japan sided with the Axis party of Germany and Italy. After the defeat of the Axis powers, Japan was forced to return Taiwan to China.

After the creation of the People's Republic of China in 1949, relationships between the two countries became more friendly. Over the next twenty years, relations remained inconsistent, sometimes friendly, sometimes not. In the 1970s, the two countries signed a friendship treaty. Since then, the relationship has continued to have its problems, but is generally growing stronger.

CHINA AND ASIA

For most of its early history, China was the leading power in Asia, both economically and technologically. Many periods existed, however, when Japan was considered the major power of the area. Today, both countries are important forces in the region. However, China is being called on increasingly to use its unique position as the leading Communist power in the world, and a major economic power, to influence other countries, both in and outside Asia.

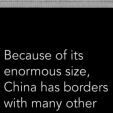

capital city
country border

ARCTIC OCEAN

Chukchi Sea — Bering Strait

East Siberian Sea

Bering Sea

Kara Sea

Laptev Sea

EUROPE

RUSSIA

Sea of Okhotsk

Astana ⊛
KAZAKHSTAN

Ulan Bator ⊛
MONGOLIA

Sea of Japan

JAPAN
Tokyo ⊛

NORTH KOREA

UZBEKISTAN

⊛ P'yongyang

Ashgabat ⊛   Tashkent ⊛ Bishkek
⊛   KYRGYZSTAN
TURKMENISTAN   ⊛ Dushanbe
TAJIKISTAN

Beijing ⊛

Seoul ⊛ SOUTH KOREA

Yellow Sea

Caspian Sea

CHINA

East China Sea

⊛ Taipei

TAIWAN

PACIFIC OCEAN

0   500   1,000 miles

0   500   1,000 kilometers

Because of its enormous size, China has borders with many other countries.

North Korea

China's position as the leading Communist country in the world is especially important to its relationship with North Korea. North Korea is another Communist country in Asia. China and North Korea have enjoyed a long, if uneven, friendship. As the smaller power, North Korea is economically dependent on China. China depends on North Korea as a friendly country on its **border**. North Korea provides a buffer between China and the democratic country of South Korea.

North Korea has a difficult relationship with most of the major powers of the world. The North Korean leader, Kim Jong-Il, is seen as untrustworthy and unpredictable. This makes China an especially important ally. China's success depends on Asia being a peaceful continent, so China wants North Korea to get along better with other countries.

In the fall of 2007, China helped North Korea meet with five other countries (the United States, China, South Korea, Japan, and Russia) to discuss North Korea's weapons program. The agreement made at the meeting is seen widely as a victory for China as it won international respect.

Myanmar (Burma)

One recent example of China's changing role in Asia is related to the small country of Myanmar (Burma). Since the 1980s, Myanmar has been ruled by a **military dictatorship**. China is an important economic partner for the smaller country. In 2007, Buddhist **monks** began a large, peaceful protest in Myanmar. The military government reacted violently to the protest. Many countries **condemned** these actions. China, which had not previously spoken against the government in other similar cases, came under pressure to state its disapproval. China joined with other members of the **United Nations** to demand that the government listen to the protesters.

This photograph shows monks protesting in the streets during 2007.

Mount Kailash is one of the holiest sites in Tibet.

Tibet

Tibet is a small area inside China. It is located on a plateau that is surrounded by mountains. People in Tibet practice a form of Buddhism. They believe strongly in **reincarnation**. From 1911–1950, Tibet was an independent country. In 1950, China invaded Tibet, claiming that its leader, the Dalai Lama, ruled unfairly. The Dalai Lama is both the religious and political ruler of Tibet. In 1959, the current Dalai Lama, worried about his safety, left Tibet for India. Today, he is a very popular figure around the world.

The Dalai Lama was chosen when he was a young boy. He has said that the next Dalai Lama will not be born inside China, but in a free country.

Struggles over Tibet

Officially, Tibet is an autonomous region, which means that it rules itself. However, the Chinese government still tries to control the area. Human rights groups around the world have called China's rule of the area a horrible abuse of human rights. In 2007, the Chinese government took a very strange action. It said that any Buddhist monks living outside China are not allowed to be reincarnated. It also claimed that the government would choose the next Dalai Lama, not Tibetan monks, as is traditional. The Dalai Lama's popularity is responsible for much of the protest around the world against the Chinese government's practices in Tibet. The Chinese government is trying to lessen the Dalai Lama's popularity, and make sure that his successor is not as popular.

Sudan

China also is being called to change its actions in other places around the world. Sudan, a country in Africa, has been dealing with a **civil war** for decades. The violence has left the country very unsafe. China has a lot of money invested in Sudan's oil industry. While many countries in the rest of the world have tried to find a solution to the Sudan crisis, China often has been accused of using its power to prevent other countries from solving the crisis. China also sells weapons to the Sudanese government. Many of these weapons have been used against the Sudanese people, particularly in the region of Darfur. However, in 2007, China began to come under pressure to use its economic power to influence the Sudanese government. The situation remains unchanged.

China has been criticized for not helping to end the crisis in Sudan.

Changes Inside China

One of the clearest examples of China's growing power in the world is its successful bid to host the 2008 Summer Olympics. Hosting the Olympics puts a country in the spotlight not only for the time of the games, but for the time it takes to prepare for the games as well. This new attention on China has called for many changes to everyday Chinese culture.

The Olympic Games are a symbol of peace and cooperation. Many people wonder if China, a country that does not always treat its own people fairly, is an appropriate place to hold the Olympics.

Four new pests

As part of its preparation for the games, China is trying to improve public manners. During Mao's government, people spoke of the "four pests," rats, flies, mosquitoes, and sparrows. Today there are "four new pests," spitting, cutting in line, swearing, and smoking. The government is working on campaigns to get Chinese citizens to have better manners. A 2006 survey seemed to show that the campaigns are working. People are spitting in public less, and taxi drivers are seen as more polite.

For China, The Special Olympics acted as a dress rehearsal for the 2008 World Olympics.

THE SPECIAL OLYMPICS

In October 2007, Shanghai became the second city outside the United States to host the World Summer Special Olympics. The Special Olympics are a sports competition for children with intellectual disabilities. China's economic growth has been very uneven. In some places, people are very wealthy. In others, they are quite poor. The Chinese government hoped that hosting the Special Olympics would help begin a culture of being compassionate to people. It was hoped that this compassion would help unify the country.

History vs. change

In China, politics and culture are tied together. When the Communists took over China, they attempted to change the culture dramatically. However, they also wanted to maintain China's pride in its history. As China has become more and more open to the rest of the world, this has changed its culture as well.

Religion

Under Mao, many places of worship in China were closed or destroyed. Today, religious groups are allowed to operate within very strict rules. The ancient Chinese **philosophies** of **Confucianism** and **Daoism** are practiced widely. Religions from other countries, such as **Islam**, Buddhism, and **Christianity**, also are practiced. Christianity has grown in recent years, but many Christians are **persecuted**. Many people practice a combination of religions. For example, they follow ancient Chinese practices regarding **ancestors**, but also visit Buddhist temples.

China has more than 13,000 Buddhist temples.

Falun Gong

In the 1990s, a new religion, Falun Gong, developed out of Buddhism. At first, the Chinese government supported the practice. However, by 1999, the Chinese government had banned the religion. Amnesty International, and other human rights groups, claim that the Chinese persecute and harm followers of Falun Gong. It is believed that 100 million people around the world practice Falun Gong. In other countries, followers of the religion frequently hold protests against the Chinese government.

Falun Gong stresses truthfulness, compassion, and patience.

A CHANGE IN ATTITUDE

According to the traditional Chinese calendar, the year that started in 2007 was "The Year of the Pig." The Chinese government ordered that out of respect for its Muslim population, companies should not have commercials featuring pigs. Muslims consider pigs unclean. This respect for a minority within China is a new position for the government.

Food

Chinese cooking is one of the oldest styles of cooking in the world. Traditionally, meals consist of rice, noodles, or bread served with several small portions of vegetable and fish dishes. Meat is eaten only in small portions. Chinese people eat with chopsticks. While Chinese food can be found around the world, foods from other parts of the world also can be found in China. This introduction of new foods to the country is changing not only people's eating habits, but also their health.

These traditional Chinese ingredients can be found in most grocery stores around the world. Food is just one of the many things that China has influenced around the world.

Obesity

China's first official nutrition survey, released in 2004, showed that people were becoming overweight in alarming numbers. In large cities, 12 percent of adults and 8 percent of children were classified as obese. The government said this was due to eating too much fat and not getting enough exercise. These are problems experienced around the world. Jobs today are less physical than jobs in the past. For example, working at a desk, as many Chinese people do, does not burn as many calories as picking rice by hand, as many Chinese people used to do.

In the 1980s, fast-food restaurants began opening in China. The first McDonald's opened in Shenzhen in 1990. A survey in 2004 found that 41 percent of Chinese people eat at a fast-food restaurant at least once a week. The same survey found that 35 percent of Americans ate at a fast-food restaurant at least once a week. McDonald's is one of several American fast-food chains that is successful in China. Sales of McDonald's are now growing faster in China than in the United States.

Fast-food restaurants offer Chinese people a taste of American culture.

Sports

Physical activity always has been important in China. What we today call martial arts probably originated in China and India. Today, different forms of these sports are practiced around the world. Sports from other countries also are practiced in China.

Basketball

Yao Ming is one of the most popular Chinese athletes both in China and the United States. Ming, who is 7 feet 6 inches (2.29 meters) tall, originally played with a team in the Chinese Basketball Association (CBA). He now plays for the U.S. National Basketball Association (NBA). He has helped make basketball more popular in China, where he is considered a national hero. His move from the CBA to the NBA helped start a new Chinese/American sports exchange.

Yao Ming is a symbol of how Chinese and American sports are changing each other.

It is believed that a sport similar to soccer was first played in China in 50 BCE.

Soccer

Soccer (known as football in China) is one of the most popular Western sports. It was first introduced to the country in 1900. In 1999, the Chinese women's team finished second in the World Cup. In 2002, they were runners up in the Olympics. The Chinese men's team qualified for the World Cup, but did not do very well in the competition. Soccer is one of the most popular sports around the world. Its growing importance in China is one more example of how China and the rest of the world are coming closer and closer together.

Changes Ahead?

Changes in China are watched carefully around the world, because of the country's huge size. The Chinese government has ambitious economic plans. Many people in the West worry that China will gain too much economic power. They fear that this will cause China to replace the United States as the major economic force in the world.

Other people throughout the world worry that China's strict government will cause further unrest in the country. As Chinese people become more exposed to Western-style democracy, they will want these freedoms for themselves. How will the government handle this?

People inside China wonder about the changes ahead as well. Will generations of children born under the One Child Policy be able to care for their aging parents and grandparents? Will the growing economic divide between poor and rich Chinese people make people more compassionate or less understanding? How will China solve its environmental problems, such as pollution and smog?

For centuries, China remained hidden from the world. For centuries after that, it remained little-understood. Today, while China and the rest of the world are getting to know each other better, the future remains a mystery.

As the Chinese people become richer and better educated, will they demand more political rights in the future?

Many Chinese cities are overcrowded, leading to pollution and other health issues. How will this affect China's growth?

Timeline

1900	The Boxer Rebellion takes place.
1911	Revolution sweeps away China's last imperial dynasty.
1912	The Republic of China is proclaimed with Sun Zhongshan as its provisional president, soon replaced by Yuan Shikai. The Nationalist Party is founded, with Sun Yatsen as its chairman.
1949	Communist troops capture Beijing and Nanjing. The People's Republic of China is established, with Mao Zedong as its leader.
1950	Red Army invades Tibet. China and the USSR sign a friendship treaty. China enters the Korean War.
1953	China launches the Five Year Plan.
1960	Widespread famine marks the Great Leap Forward's end. The USSR withdraws all advisers from China.
1972	U.S. President Nixon visits China.
1976	The death of Zhou Enlai triggers Tiananmen Square demonstrations. Mao Zedong dies.
1978	Deng Xiaoping emerges as leader.
1984	China and Britain issue a joint declaration on the future of Hong Kong.
1989	Pro-democracy demonstrations end bloodily in Tiananmen Square.

1997   Deng Xiaoping dies.
Hong Kong is returned to Chinese control by Britain.

2001   China joins the World Trade Organization.

2002   The government tries to cover up an outbreak of SARS in China.

2007   There are several scandals involving contamination of pet food
and toys made in China.
China helps create a weapons agreement with North Korea.
China hosts the World Summer Special olympics.

2008   China hosts the 2008 Summer Olympics.

Glossary

ancestor someone who lived before you in your family, who is dead now

authoritarian extremely strict form of government that does not allow disagreement

birth rate the number of births within a population

border division between two countries

Buddhism religion based on the teachings of the Buddha

capitalist economy based on the idea that the market will decide what is and is not valuable; person who believes this is the best government

censorship act of preventing people from expressing ideas and opinions

Christianity religion based on the teachings of Jesus Christ

civil war war between two parties within the same country

collapse break apart

Communist government based on the teachings of Karl Marx; person who believes in the teachings of Marx

condemn make a judgement against

Confucianism belief system started by Confucius

culture actions and beliefs of a society

Daoism religion based on the ideas of Laozi

democratic where the government has been elected by the people

dialect variety of a language that is spoken in a particular region

dynasty families that rule an area for more than one generation

economic relating to the economy, a country's system of buying and selling goods and all of the things that it makes and buys

emperor ruler who has total power, like a king

export sell items to other countries

famine time when there is not enough food for everyone

imperial to do with the emperor

import bring items into a country to sell

Industrial Revolution movement that started in Great Britain in the 18th century that changed the economy of many countries

industry business of making goods in factories

Islam religion based on the teachings of the prophet Mohammed

isolated separated from others

market-based economy economy based on the idea that the buyers and sellers in a country will decide naturally how much goods should cost and how much people should be paid for services

military dictatorship form of government where the ruler has taken over with the help of the army and has unlimited power

monk male member of a religion living in a special way, apart from other people

Nationalist one of two political parties in the 1900s in China

peasant worker who works on land raising food, but does not own the land

persecution unfair punishment

philosophy way of thinking about the world

political related to the way a country is run or its government

reincarnation belief that after death, people are reborn as other people or animals

revolutionary involved in a revolution, such as a complete change of government

SARS virus that affects the lungs and can be deadly

Soviet Union group of communist countries, led by Russia, which existed from 1922 to 1991; also known as the USSR

technology scientific knowledge used in practical ways

totalitarian form of government that demands people believe and obey one set of ideas

United Nations organization of the world's countries to keep peace and order internationally

World Trade Organization (WTO) international organization designed to administer trade between countries

Further Information

Books

Field, Catherine. *Nations of the World: China*. Chicago: Raintree, 2003.

Guile, Melanie. *Culture in China*. Chicago: Heinemann, 2003.

March, Michael. *Country File: China*. North Mankato, MN: Smart Apple
Media, 2004.

Olson, Nathan. *China*. Mankato, MN: Capstone, 2005.

Places to visit

Many U.S. cities have an area of town known as "Chinatown." These areas specialize in Chinese restaurants, grocery stores, and clothing stores as well as other businesses owned by Chinese Americans. Some of the more famous Chinatowns are located in San Francisco, Chicago, and New York. If you are planning a trip to one of these cities you can find the Chinatown chamber of commerce on the Internet.

Many museums have good Chinese collections. Here are some of the more famous ones:

The Metropolitan Museum of Art
1000 5th Ave at 82nd Street
New York, NY 10028-0198
(212) 535-7710 www.metmuseum.org

The Field Museum
1201 S Lake Shore Dr
Chicago, IL 60605
(312) 665-7909 www.fieldmuseum.org

Asian Art Museum of San Francisco
200 Larkin Street
San Francisco, CA 94102
(415) 581-3500 www.asianart.org

Seattle Asian Art Museum
1400 East Prospect Street
Seattle, WA 98112
(206) 654-3100 www.seattleartmuseum.org

Websites

Ask Asia
www.askasia.org/kids/
This website provides information for students and teachers on
Asian countries.

Official Chinese government website
www.china.org.cn/english/index.htm
This official website is for English speakers. This website presents only the
images and information about China that the Chinese government wants
outsiders to see.

The CIA Factbook
**https://www.cia.gov/library/publications/the-world-factbook/geos/
ch.html**
The CIA factbook has information on every country in the world. This website
is run by the U.S. government.